Folk Tales
for Children

GOPU
BOOKS

An Imprint of V&S PUBLISHERS

Published by:

An Imprint of

F-2/16, Ansari Road, Daryaganj, New Delhi-110002
☎ 011-23240026, 011-23240027 • *Fax:* 011-23240028
Email: info@vspublishers.com • *Website:* www.vspublishers.com

Regional Office : Hyderabad
5-1-707/1, Brij Bhawan (Beside Central Bank of India Lane)
Bank Street, Koti, Hyderabad - 500 095
☎ 040-24737290
E-mail: vspublishershyd@gmail.com

Follow us on:

For any assistance sms **VSPUB** to **56161**

All books available at **www.vspublishers.com**

© **Copyright:** V&S PUBLISHERS
ISBN 978-93-505708-6-9
Edition 2014

Printed at : Param Offseters, Okhla, New Delhi-110020

publisher's note

V&S Publishers has been in the forefront in publishing story books for children - under the imprint Gopu Books. Most books are educational, moral and value-based in nature. Nearly every book published under this imprint has been lapped up by parents and guardians on behalf of their children, both in English and Hindi versions. Since the dawn of time, parents have used stories with morals to teach children about the values of the family, about life, difference between right and wrong, good and bad. A story with a moral can help, more so contemporary ones with which children can relate conveniently. Unlike most prevalent books in the market that exist only for their entertainment value, this book **Folk Tales for Children** offers to build strength of character and respect for others.

This book is a compilation of 50 one-page stories for children. Language used is elementary and simple. Each story comes with caricature based illustration in black & white – a presentation no other publisher has attempted before. Being different from the ordinary run of the mills type, the caricatures retain interest of young readers. The moral at the end of the story summaries precisely what the child is supposed to learn!

By reading stories, children will gather how characters deal with situations and work through issues, they gain experience without having to go through those conditions themselves. Their outlook is broadened that fits the ethos and mores of a traditional society like ours.

We would be glad to receive feedback from parents so that future publications retain the flavour of enlightened views that expand horizon of our young readers.

----

contents

the half-eaten feast

In the state of Rajasthan there was a town called Dhanpuri. A person called 'Jeevta Maharaj' used to live in this town. He was known as a big glutton. One day the news reached Jeevta Maharaj that, a wealthy person in the town called Seth Dhannamal was blessed with a grandson; therefore to celebrate the child's birth a feast was hosted in the town. Even without an invitation Jeevta Maharaj went there to enjoy the feast. He sat amidst a row of people and started eating the grand meal. First row of people got over, second arrived to eat and rose and so on... Even the tenth row of people was also done with the feast. But Jeevta Maharaj kept on eating. After seeing him eat Dhannamal got a bit worried, he thought now two things may happen, first the food might fall short or second the elderly Jeevta Maharaj might die and he will be sinned for it, for rest of his life. With all his concern he went and stood right in front of Jeevta Maharaj and said, 'Maharaj please drink this water now'.

To that Jeevta Maharaj said, 'oh Danna you are so kind. It is my habit to drink water after finishing one-fourth of my meal.' By saying this he gulped all the water in one go. Seeing this Dhannamal said, 'Maharaj how much more will you eat now?' Jeevta Maharaj replied 'till it pleases my appetite I will keep on eating'. 'If you don't want me to eat further I can get up from this feast empty stomach.' Dhannamal saw fifteen rows of people got over with eating this grand meal, but Dhanna Maharaj was now lying flat at the place where he was sitting. His breathing had slowed down, and his body started trembling. Dhannamal ran toward him and asked in great worry, 'Jeevta Maharaj! Are you alive or not?' To which he said 'this is the satisfaction of my half-filled stomach only. I am still alive and I wish you also live a good life Dhanna.' After listening to this Dhannamal got the clue it sums up to only half of the meal of the great glutton Jeevta Maharaj therefore he is going to eat more now. After this Dhannamal did not knock him more and asked all his stewarts to keep on serving Jeevta Maharaj because without his appetite being satiated the celebration of the birth of his grandson will not be complete.

Virtues of Hospitality

*I*n a village far away there lived a very poor man whose name was Sukhiya. He could earn only that much so that he could survive it for a day. Nobody had ever seen discontentment and distress ever on his face. One fine evening Sukhiya was having supper with his family. Someone knocked at his door. It was a traveller; he had lost his way and came to his village on his way to his distination. Sukhiya welcomed this stranger, now a guest in his home, and offered him some food, while doing so he gave his entire share of food to his guest. After eating the small amount of food given the guest's appetite was not satiated. Therefore his wife and children gave their share of food to this guest as well. After eating and getting his appetite satiated the guest showed interest in sleeping in his house overnight.

In the morning when Sukhiya was worrying about the breakfast to be given to his guest he noticed his guest had already left without telling anyone. Sukhiya felt a bit strange with his guest's behaviour but he decided to leave for his work. All of a sudden a royal carriage came in front of his house and stopped right there. During that night the man who arrived happened to be the King, he came as a traveller after changing his kingly dress because by doing so he could see how well his subjects lived in his kingdom. He came out of his carriage and held Sukhiya close to his heart because he was happy to see there are people in his country that could give away their food to honour a guest and still remained content in life. He showed his gratitude for offering him his own food also. King asked Sukhiya's entire family to come to his palace and dine with him; he also offered a place to Sukhiya so that he can serve his king in his palace forever.

Moral

For extending courtesy and showing good virtues to a guest can earn one greater and sweeter rewards.

fluid wealth

Once upon a time in Rampur village a business man lived. His name was Munjimal. One day in his dream Goddess Lakshmi appeared. The Goddess said, 'I can stay no longer with you so I have to go now.' And the business man got really worried in his dream. He told his wife about his dream. His wife suggested only good deeds and giving alms could make Goddess remain with us. It was our good fate that she chose us for such a long time and stayed with us. But Munjimal was a very miser person. To give away his wealth in alms that too to poor people was not his nature. He wanted to grab hold of Laskhmi and never let her go. He was hell bent that he would never let go of Lakshmi ever. He came up with an idea to make Lakshmi stay with him. Lakshmi did tell him that she wants to go out of his house now. Munjimal bore a whole in a tree trunk and stuffed it with all his precious ornaments and gold coins. After stuffing tree bark with all his wealth he kept it outside his house. After seeing all this, his wife spoke, 'whatever efforts you will make but it will not stop Lakshmi for going where she wants to go at her will.' The business man said, 'when she is not living in the house and she is sitting right outside in a tree trunk, now where she can go.'

All day long Munjimal took care of tree trunk. He stayed awake till mid night but then he fell asleep. During the same time it rained quite heavily. That tree trunk went floating towards the shack of a poor man and stopped there. There a poor man lived called 'Birma'. He thought maybe God has sent fire wood to him in order to burn it. He dragged that tree trunk inside his shack. The very moment he tried to chop fire wood a huge amount of wealth came pouring out of the trunk. When Munjimal woke up he went almost mad looking for his Lakshmi everywhere. When Birma heard Munjimal crying loud he told him the entire story and asked him to come to his shack and take away his wealth from there.

When Munjimal realised what has happened in the form of this miracle, he folded his hands in prayer and said, 'God you told us right that wealth is fluid its flow never stays stagnant anywhere.' Munjimal immediately gave away his wealth to Birma and other poor man around him and started arranging for a new welcome for the Lakshmi to enter his house again.

Moral

Wealth is ever changing; one cannot make it remain as it is forever.

a precious grain of rice

*O*nce upon a time Lord Ganesha had turned himself into a small child. He then held a spoon full of milk in one hand and his other hand was holding only one grain of rice. He would go to every house and request people to make Kheer for him. All the women could not help themselves from laughing after seeing a spoon full of milk and a grain of rice in his hands. They would say 'how can one ever make kheer out of this alone?' when the child would start giving tantrums some women would turn him away by telling him something or the other or some would get angry and tell the child to leave.

It was evening and the child finally reached a small hut, where an old woman used to live. This child requested the old woman by saying, 'oh dear mother please make kheer for me- I have been to several places and palaces, I have milk and rice both with me. I do not know what a hard work it is that no one can make it for me even when I give them ingredients as well.' The old woman kissed the child lovingly and said, 'oh dearly beloved! Let me make kheer for you.' She asked her daughter in law to 'bring a small pot so that she can make kheer.' Now the child had a different trick in his mind that whichever pot is the biggest in the house he wants the kheer to be made in it. The old woman agreed to his tantrum and started preparing kheer in the biggest pot in her house and the child started playing outside.

When she put a spoon full of milk and one grain of rice the entire pot was filled with it to the brim suddenly. The pot was full of milk and rice. Everyone was amazed to see this. The old woman kept on looking for the small child but she could not find him after looking through the entire village. When the daughter in law saw the delicious kheer she hid a cup full of it and said her graces to God and had it. When she was roaming around to find that child all of a sudden a voice wad heard, 'Mother! I have tasted your delicious kheer when I was hiding behind the door and had a cup full of it. Now give a feast to the entire village so that they also enjoy this kheer.' While feeding every one the old woman could not help but recite, 'after making kheer of one grain of rice and spoon full of milk .' God hase given me enough kheer to feed the entire village. Even palace dwellers could not help but be grateful to the Lord when they were feasting on this old woman's kheer.

Moral

When God desires then even a single grain of rice and a spoon full of milk can be sufficient for the entire village to satisfy their hunger.

to take and to give

There was a very miser business man who saw a bad dream one night. He saw that his wealth in the form of Goddess Lakshmi was leaving him. The business man was disturbed by this dream and could not sleep at all. He woke up his wife and told her everything. But his wife was a very clever woman. She said to him not to worry and get some sleep for now. In the morning we will see what this dream was about. After getting up in the morning she immediately started giving her jewellery and money to the poor people. So much so that she gave away her mansion where they lived for charity to make a lodge for travellers there.

When the business man asked her what she was doing, she said it is all pointless because Lakshmi is going to leave them now. So why not use it properly. So the business man also agreed what fate decides no one can alter it. All day this giving away business went on, people would come empty handed and would go with something or the other. The day was ended and the night fell. To start everything fresh they pledged and slept calmly.

After mid night Lakshmi came in the man's dream again and spoke, 'I will never abandon you and will never leave you.' The business man could not understand anything but she said, 'where there is charity and giving I never leave such a place.' The very next day business man received news of profit in his trade. And he recovered all his wealth which he gave away. He understood what one gives from one hand comes back from another. So no one returned empty handed from his doorstep ever.

It is always good to offer things to the needy or engage in charity. Goddess Lakshmi resides in people who have a charitable bent of mind.

Moral

Where there is charity and selfless giving, wealth never leaves such a place.

worry

In a village there were two houses. One house belonged to a poor milkman Bholu and the other belonged to a very wealthy businessman Ramcharan. Despite being poor, Bholu was a very cheerful person. He didn't need to shut his doors and windows before sleeping at night. On the other hand, Ramcharan was always tense. He had so many worries to look after. To hum a tune was a different matter. He hardly ever laugh out openly with others due to his worries. He would shut his doors and windows at night but could never manage a sound sleep. He started feeling jealous of Bholu.

One day Ramcharan called Bholu to his house and asked him 'please keep my money safe in your house. Consider this money as yours. And you do not have to return this money back to me.' To receive so much of money Bholu was very happy. He took the money and went back to his home. The money should not get stolen this is why he first time closed his doors and windows. To see whether all his money is secure he woke up several times during night. He was unable to get a sound sleep. Whenever he would go out of the house he remained concerned and worried about the security of his money.

For a long time this kept on going, after which Bholu took all the money and went straight to Ramcharan's house and said, 'Sir, please take all this money back and keep it with you. This money has destroyed my sleep and peace. I have forgotten simple joys of life like singing and laughing. Worry of protecting so much of wealth is disturbing me day and night. I do not wish to have such a wealth, I do not want money which will increase my worry further and take away my happiness. At least I was better to do even when I was poor'.

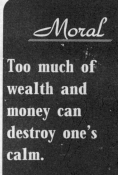

Moral

Too much of wealth and money can destroy one's calm.

Few comforting words

There was a beggar, whatever he could get after begging he would survive on it only. One day while begging he reached a wealthy man's mansion. The beggar stopped at the gate and started calling for alms. The mansion guard yelled at him and shoved him away saying 'go away from this place.' The guard scolded him again 'go from this place right now', but beggar has spread both his arms and kept on asking for alms.

All of a sudden he saw the wealthy man's accountant was coming there. Beggar raised his voice and asked to give something at least to him. Hearing his loud voice the accountant got enraged and said 'you beggars have no shame is asking for money? You become have accustomed to begging and feeding on such a life.'

After saying this accountant left the place. The beggar still thought that he might get something if he will stand there for some time more. In a while the wealthy man came himself. He saw beggar standing there and started to scold his guard at the door 'tell him to leave this place.' Before this beggar could speak the guard pushed him away. The beggar turned around and saw the big mansion and mumbled such a big house and so much of poverty. No money to give but they cannot offer few words of comfort either.

The better felt sad that despite having enormous wealth, they had no heart, no feeling for other people's pain. he wondered what's the use of such wealth when it can't feed even one singh soul.

Saying so he thought if only he had money he would pave fed people and given alms to the needy.

He understood the dignity of labour. he started working and in no time become prosperous. He started feeding the needy. If gave him happiness.

Moral

Even if there is nothing to offer to someone but one can sooth the person with few kind words.

duty of a sailor

*F*ew people were travelling in a boat they were going to a certain place together. Suddenly a storm came and it started to rain heavily. All the passengers panicked. The frenzy struck everyone in a hurry. The sailor decided to put his vessel ashore but in storm he could not manage to do so. Even then he did not let go of his courage. Despite the fact he was much tired he dragged his body to work and tried to take his boat reach the shore.

Slowly the water started to enter his boat. All passengers were busy putting out water from this boat. But water level was rising in the boat. Sailor was not able to bear strong current of waves. He was disappointed and he left the oars and bowed down holding his head in his hands. Within few moments everyone on the boat lost their lives and the boat got sunk. After his death the sailor was dragged to hell and all the while he was asking what his sin was. Yam Raj replied 'you have sinned because of you all the passengers of the boat died.'

Sailor was startled and spoke 'this is no justice. I tried so hard to save my boat and the passengers on it. But the storm was strong. What I could have done alone?' Yam Raj replied 'this is correct that you worked hard, but you did not perform your duty completely, because you left rowing your own boat mid way. It was your duty to have rowed it till the end. You were solely responsible for the passenger's life.' Having heard Yam Raj speak the sailor realised his fault and agreed he was responsible for his act.

Moral

One must perform one's duty till the end.

four wives

A businessman had four wives. He used to love his fourth wife the most. He would buy her precious jewellery, bear all her tantrums, and fulfil all her wishes. He also loved his third wife. He would always introduce her to all his friends. But the business man was scared that someday she might leave him and go away. He also loved the second wife equally well. She was very clever and smart. Whenever business man had a doubt he would seek opinion from his second wife. But this businessman seldom loved her first wife. She was a very dedicated wife. In his tough times she had helped him a lot.

One day businessman fell ill. He started reflecting on his life, 'all my life I lived with four wives but today I will die alone.' So he asked his fourth wife now that I am dying would you come with me?'

She refused bluntly and without saying anything she left that place. He asked the same question to his third wife. Third wife replied 'never, I am very happy here. After your death I will marry again.' Now he asked his second wife. When I die will you come with me she replied 'forgive me this time I will not be able to help you. Listening to this the businessman was totally shattered. Then a voice came, 'I will come with you.' The businessman saw his first wife was standing in front of him. 'I should have paid a lot of attention towards you.'

If you see we all have four wives in our lives. The fourth wife is our own body. No matter how much time we spend on it, when we die it leaves us immediately. Third wife is our money when we die it goes to others. And second wife is our family and children. When we die they go till funeral pyre after that we are alone. And the first wife is our soul which we tend to neglect it for the wealth and opulence. Despite everything and every neglect it remains with us forever. We must learn to respect it on time; else we will regret it later.

it's a wonderful world

One day Rehmat Miyan went out and got dressed in his best dress, he wore a perfect cap, a silken shirt, teamed with a very majestic stick in his hand. Shoes from Sholapur was complimenting his attire very much. He was walking in a happy mood then Rehmat thought, why not go to the mosque first and pray then he will go further. He took his shoes off and went inside. After his prayer he came outside. His eyes remained wide open to see something. His shoes were not there. He looked around but nothing was to be seen.

While Rehmat started mumbling his complains to God about what kind of people he has created in his world, who steal other people's things. And also they are not ashamed of such acts. All of a sudden he heard few words falling in his ears, 'Please give some money sir.' When he looked back in anger he saw a beggar was standing there. That beggar had one leg missing. Rehmat asked the beggar, 'why do you not have one leg brother? Do you have no complain with God that why he chose you for this act?' beggar spoke 'Sir, all I can say is how I must thank him, because his world is a wonderful place to live, he gives to all of us as his creation he looks after us and no one is empty handed here.'

To see such a shine of hope and trust in the beggar's eyes Rehmat asked for forgiveness from God within his heart. He gave money to this beggar and went ahead. While on his way he thought that he has only lost his shoes which he can buy later as well. Even then he was complaining to God for them whereas that beggar had only one leg and he will never get another. But he has no complain to make or has any remorse to tell to God. He looked towards the vast sky smiling and said 'really your world is a wonderful place to live in'.

Whatever God has given has some meaning contained within it. He has not created anything or does any work which is meaningless. We should therefore be grateful to Him that He has given us brain with which we can achieve anything we desire.

Moral

Every work of God is full of wonder and is always justified.

cleverness of budhiram

There was a wealthy merchant who lived in a village. His name was Hoshiyarmal. There was a neem tree in front of Hoshiyarmal's house. This provided a lot of shade. One day a labour sat under this dense tree to take rest. While sitting under the tree he fell asleep. His name was Budhiram. As soon as Budhiram woke up he has found that merchant was standing all most near his chest and he was asking for money from him because he has rested under his shady tree. He said 'this tree is right in front of my house that is why its shadow also belongs to me. And if you have rested right under it then pay the cost for it.'

Budhiram understood that merchant was showing his cleverness. In return Budhiram said 'mercahnt its shadow was really soothing. I desire to rest here every day. Do me a favour of selling its shadow to me.' The merchant thought that what a fool has come in his trap. Rather than getting a rent for taking a nap under his tree Hoshiyarmal decided to sell him the shadow of his tree entirely for some money and came home feeling very happy. Since then Budhiram would come running to rest under his tree all the time. The merchant would see him every day and would laugh at his foolishness.

One day with time the tree's shadow also changed its direction and it started falling on the house of this merchant. So Budhiram started to rest right next to the merchant's house and he slept there while snoring loudly. By the time evening arrived the shadow of this tree moved towards the merchant's kitchen, and then Budhiram went to get the shade inside his kitchen and sat there while eating a meal. When his wife saw this entire act she said to her husband now to show more of his cleverness! Now what the merchant could say to this Budhiram because his all cleverness had gone for a six. After this incidence he literally held his ears and asked for forgives to Budhiram. He returned his money back to him with double profit.

Moral

With cleverness and brain one can teach a lesson to even the shrewdest people.

appreciation of a skill

In a town a potter lived who used to make utensils and toys out of clay. His name was 'Madhav'. He was really skilled. All the toys he used to sculpt with his hands and clay were so real as if they can speak. With the passage of time Madhav's skill also grew fine with it. To keep utensils sculpted by Madhav was considered a prestigious matter. To see his appreciation and popularity Madhav felt very proud.

One day someone told Madhav in plain talk that, 'Madhav! Now it seems you are creating your own universe since you are so skilled in sculpting. What is missing from your work is life rest is so real.' Madhav sat that day to work, and all day long this thought kept floating in his head that he is brilliantly skilled now and what toys he has made look real now. He would try to work with more dexterity, but something was lacking in his work that day. Even people who took his clay pots started complaining that his pots have started to leek and cannot contain liquids in them. Even the moulds which were filled with clay were lacking something in their concept. Like before right kind of shapes were not coming any more. Madhav became less popular now.

After remaining affected he decided to tell this matter to his wife. While speaking he said, 'it feels as if someone's bad intentions have destroyed my skill and ability, now no work comes out well.' Madhav's wife was a smart person. She said, 'a real talent and skill gets destroyed by pride. To appreciate one's skill is great matter. It encourages the artist so much but in your heart there is so much of overconfidence due to your own pride that now you are distancing yourself from your own greatness and skill.' Now Madhav understood every detail, and once again Madhav started creating his amazing toys just as he used to in earlier times.

It is truly said that one must take pride in his work but avoid becoming proud. Proudness invariably leads to downfall.

Moral

One must not get persuaded by fake pretence or pride.

a lucky pot

In the town of Devnagri there was a man called 'Falku' who was the king's favourite and most trusted court member. With his cleverness he had impressed king several times. One day king decided to play a joke on Falku and in his court announced he will be rewarding him with a copper vessel. All the court members started to laugh, then Falku replied, 'It is my great luck and I am humbled by king's gesture that he is giving me a copper pot.' Immediately in the royal court the vessel was brought and was bestowed upon Falku. And Falku opened his sash which was tied around his waist. He tried to cover his copper pot with it and decided to carry it away.

King was still laughing and said, 'Falku why are you trying to cover the pot?' Falku replied, 'Sir, I told you that it is my great luck because of which you have bestowed such an honour on me. And I am trying to cover it because no one should know what king has given is empty from inside so that you do not have to bear any embarrassment.' After hearing such intelligent remark of Falku king got really happy. He smiled and said 'Falku's lucky pot will not go empty today; therefore it should be filled with gold coins.' And the lucky pot was filled to the brim with gold coins.

Falku again covered it with a cloth, now king asked 'why did you cover it now?' He replied 'so that no one will cast an evil eye on my great luck and king will keep on bestowing his generosity on me further that is why I covered it.' And king again in his heart applauded Falku's intelligence.

With his intelligence Falku could convince the king that the gifted item should not be empty. This is a practice followed in Indian society.

Moral

A clever mind is always entitled to any reward.

mother's pilgrim

In the Rampur village an old woman lived. When all women would go for a pilgrimage and return back they would go to this old lady and narrate their experience of worshiping God to her. And this old lady would listen to their tales with a lot of longing. One day while this old lady was sleeping she woke up from deep sleep and started to plead God for giving her a chance to go out on a pilgrimage, or else her whole life would go waste. She said, 'Oh Lord! Why don't you want me to come to you because I can barely walk and reach to you with the help of my stick? I do not know what all places I should go?' she kept on repeating these words then suddenly something fell and sounds started coming from her kitchen.

There was no one living with the old lady in her house. Her son was gone to bring had his wife from her mother's home. When she heard a sound in her kitchen she thought perhaps her son has returned home. She asked in a loud voice 'son have you come back, then why did you not come to meet me first. Will you come here or should I come?' all of a sudden another sound of window being opened came and a thief ran outside. Now the old lady understood that there was a thief in her house and he ran away because she spoke in loud voice. When she has put everything in order she found out nothing was missing and on top of it this thief had left his money tied in a bundle while running out in a hurry.

Old lady mumbled something, 'bounties of stealing were tied in a bundle, how it will suffice for a pilgrimage?' She pulled her quilt on her head and slept there saying 'God you finally came but ran away from me through a window. Now come once more and take your money with you. I have one penny with me; out of which I will buy sweets and will distribute them saying you came to my house yourself.' Thief was standing on the outer wall. He heard everything which old lady had said. He picked up his bundle and left that place but he thanked this old lady in his heart.

Moral

If one has a pure heart then every deed performed is not less than a pilgrimage itself.

farsightedness

A person named Kishanlal was very old. He had a shaky body. One day he went to the store of a jeweller called Banvari to ask for a weighing scale. Banvari said, 'I do not have a sieve.' Kishanlal said, 'maybe you have not heard properly I was asking for a weighing scale not for a sieve.' Then Banvari said, 'oh! no I do not have a broom either.' Now Kishanlal was angry at Banvari. He said 'I am asking for a weighing scale for such a long time and you are so insolent that sometime you say, you do not have a sieve or a broom, are you deaf?'

Banvari said 'I am not deaf I know what I am saying. Listen when you will measure gold dust in that weighing scale due to your shaking hands some of the gold dust might fall on the ground. Then you will come to ask for a broom at my place again. You may be able to pick all the gold dust but maybe a lot of dirt will come with it then you will need a sieve to separate the dirt from it and you will come asking for it to me. I can see from my farsightedness your work's results and that is why I was talking like that. So brother! You must ask for a weighing scale from some other shop.' After listening to him Kishanlal went across to see another shop. It is wisely said a person who keeps the results in his mind is considered as a genius.

It is truly said that the farsighted people realise an opportunity when they see one whereas the nearsighted ones overlook right under their noses.

Farsightedness or genius is not so much about new ideas as it is about clarity of ideas. Two people can have the same idea yet it will be genius in are and mediocrity in another

Moral

A person who is farsighted never gets into troubling circumstances.

friendship

Krishna and Sudama got their education from their teacher Sandeepan. They both became good friends. Later on Krishna became king of Dwarka and Sudama remained impoverished and poor.

One day Sudama's wife told him, 'Dear we have nothing in the house to eat. Your friend Krishna is Mathura's king you can ask him for help.' At Susheela's behest Sudama agreed to visit Mathura finally. His wife tied a small bag of roasted grams for him to eat. At last Sudama reached his palace.

Sudama said to guard 'I want to meet Krishna.' He replied 'call him King Krishna. He is our king'. Sudama said 'he must be king for you but to me he is my friend.'

The guard did not let him meet Krishna. He sent a message for Krishna. As soon as Krishna heard Sudama's name he came running bare feet to see him. He escorted Sudama with a lot of respect and asked him to sit on his throne. All court members were startled to see this. Sudama could not help but tears fell from his eyes. He got up to embrace Krishna. The small bag of roasted grams fell on the ground. Krishna picked it up and said 'My sister in law has sent it for me.'

The city of Dwarka treated Sudama with a lot of respect, but Krishna did not ask him once the real reason of his coming. During his departure he could not say anything to Krishna and neither Krishna asked him anything. On his entire journey Sudama was doubting Krishna's friendship. He was somewhat angry at his as well.

When he reached his place his hut was no more there. There was a very huge house standing at its place. He started to regret due to this friendship even his hut was also lost. From the roof top of that house he heard a voice, 'please enter dear it is your house itself.' This voice was of Susheela's. Sudama smiled in his heart and said for his dear friend, 'what a prankster.'

There is no difference of being small or big in any friendship. In friendship only feelings and dedication towards each other matters, like the friendship of poor Sudama and Sri Krishna.

Moral

True friendship lives in the heart; not in money.

true brotherly love

*I*n a village there lived two brothers. They were really poor. Elder brother's financial condition was better than the younger ones. But his family was quite big. They both were farmers and this is how they made their living. The time to reap their harvest was near. But the elder brother was in deep thought as how he will help his younger brother. One day the elder brother took some of the grains from his harvest and placed it neatly with the harvest of the younger brother in his storage room, so that it could help him a little bit more. But it was surprising even after giving away his share of grains, still his harvest was not reduced. For next two nights he did the same, he placed some of the food grains in his brother's store of grains. But still his crop was not depleting. He found this bit rather strange.

To learn the secret the elder brother decided to hide in his farms during the night. After few hours he saw a man was entering his storage house. The elder brother got out to see who it was. That stranger was no one other than his own younger brother. Every night his younger brother to help his elder one decided to keep some part of his produce in his storage house. So that it can ease some of his worries. After learning so much about each other the true brotherly love of both the brothers came out in open, and they lived together in harmony with each other.

There is nothing in the world which can match brotherly love. Brotherly love is unmatched and unparalleled. Brothers act as a great source of support and back-up and one can court on them in the most needed times of aid and help. Brothers are always very protective.

Moral

If brothers have true love between them then poverty does not prefigure anywhere between such brothers.

meaning of life

One day in the academy of teacher Augustus a prince arrived to acquire education. He proposed to have a dialogue with his teacher before starting the learning programme in his academy. He said 'I have few questions. And if the teacher could answer them I am ready to become his disciple. After listening to this the other students were amazed. They looked towards their teacher. But on the face of their teacher there was no anger visible. H smiled at him and said 'it is fine son now you may ask your questions.'

The prince asked 'can you tell me the sole purpose of humanity?' 'No' said the teacher. 'Alright then answer my second question' said the prince. 'What is the meaning of human life?' teacher said 'I cannot give you the answer of this question either.' Now the prince asked third most important question 'what is death? And after this life what lies ahead?' 'I do not know the answer of this question also.' The teacher replied getting agitated with the prince. And now the prince said, 'when you yourself do not know the answers of these questions then what knowledge can you impart to us. I will not come under your tutelage.' He said this much and left his academy.

After listening to him some disciples got very angry and some felt their teacher is not an educated man. And the teacher understood what all was happening inside his student's mind. He said 'how can you know all the life's complexities, the life which you all have not started yet. To see a delectable feast lying ahead of you is not wise but to analyse it by tasting it would be wiser. Which means to have seen others live their lives cannot guide you about what life is all about. Therefore try living it on your own first. Your entire question will have their answers.'

a bookish knowledge

One day Imam Ghazali was leaving on a tour to a foreign land. Right in the middle of his journey, the roads were quite desolate, where highway man used to flock. He got tired of walking. He decided to spread a sheet under a tree and took out one book from his bag pack to read. That very moment all the highway men attacked him. The head of these dacoits asked Ghazali, 'whatever wealth or money you have take it all out now, or else you will lose your life.'

Ghazali said, 'but I have my clothes and books only.' To this head of dacoits said 'your clothes and books are what use for us. But off-course one can get money after selling off these books.' Saying so this, the head snatched away Ghazali's bag of books. Ghazali pleaded him by saying, 'these books are of great use for me. To sell them away you can make only plentiful money but it will be of great loss for me. Whenever I find out something meaningful I refer to my books. If you will take them away how will I refer to them when needed the most? Have mercy on me and return my books to me.'

To hear this matter the head of all highway men dropped the bag of books on ground and said, 'what is the point of such a knowledge which never comes without books. Now take your bag away you think of yourself as a very knowledgeable man. There is no value of yours without these books.' This wisdom influenced Ghazali the most. After this Ghazali locked all the wisdom and teaching of these books in his mind. In future he became a very renowned religious leader and an Imam who was a spiritual head as well.

From your parents you learn love and laughter and how to put one foot before the other. But when books are opened, you discover that you have wings.

Imam learnt that we continue to believe that books embody the ideas that turn us from isolated souls into a powerful communicator for the betterment of society.

Moral

With the bookish knowledge it is most vital to have a practical knowledge of life as well.

power of words

*O*ne beggar was passing across a village one day. He saw a lady while walking she seemed very distressed. The beggar asked her what was the reason for her distress. The lady said her son was severely ill that is why she was sad. None of the medicines were working in his favour. The beggar asked this lady to take him at her place. When he reached there he held her son's head in his lap and started praying to God for the health of her child.

To see him doing so the boy's father grew angry at him. He said, 'what do you think with your prayers our son will get better? A lot of big doctors were not able to treat him and you think you can.' After listening to him the beggar replied 'you are one insolent fool. Keep your mouth shut and let me do what I am doing right now. You do not know anything about these matters.' To hear the beggar talk in this manner he grew even angrier at him. Before this man could utter another word the beggar placed his hand on his shoulder gently and said 'forgive me I should have not talked to you like this and what all I have said in anger'. To hear him say this, man became somewhat patient. And the beggar replied again 'think about it when my one word can make you angry and the other word can pacify you immediately then reflect when my few words will combine together in a prayer then they can heal your son as well.' That man understood what the beggar was talking about.

It is truly said that words are a form of action, capable of influencing change. Their articulation represents a complete experience. So be careful of what you say, keep them short and sweet. you never know, from day to day, which ones of your spoken words you will have to eat.

Moral

Words have a lot of potential. Good words have greater influence and bad words have similar effect on people

let it happen

*I*n a village lived a woman named Shanti. She was wealthy but very alone. She had no one in her life that she could call as her own. To overcome her loneliness she would arrange for a feast for the village every now and then. With time Shanti's body and health was deteriorating. But she still organised these feast for everyone. But finally her last day arrived. Yamdut came on earth in the disguise of a mortal to carry her soul away.

That moment in Shanti's house this feast was going on. And the whole house was brimming with cheer and happiness. And Yamdut also participated in this feast finally. He told Shanti that 'it is your time to die now. I have come here to take your soul with me.' Shanti said 'as you can see the happy ambience of my house will get destroyed.' Yamdut said 'but I have to carry hundred mortal souls today with me. You must hurry up because I cannot wait longer for you.' Shanti said 'then you can go and take those other hundred first by that time I will get over with my work and will come with you as the last one.' He replied 'but first name is yours that is why I will take you with me first.' Shanti heard him and invited him for feast, Doot accepted her invitation and sat in one corner to eat and started eating the food.

Shanti grabbed the opportunity and cut her name from the list which was written on the top and shifted it right at the bottom of it. When Doot got up from eating he agreed to follow Shanti's terms and said 'I agree with your request and I will first take other peoples soul with me then I will come for you. And now I will began with that person whose name will be the last on my list.' As soon as he saw his list Shanti's name was written last on it. Shanti just said these words last and agreed to come with him,

No one can deter, what has been written so let it be.

Whatever practices one will follow, it will happen so let it be.

Moral

God's words are absolute no one can deter or alter it.

the knowledgeable

*O*ne day a rich trader asked Lao-Tzu, 'your student Yen is better than you by what virtue?' Lao-Tzu said 'in greatness he is higher than me.' 'And your student Kung's better characteristic is what if compared with yours?' Asked the trader. Lao-Tzu said 'his voice is sweeter than mine for sure.' The trader asked again 'your disciple Chang is better in which sense?' Lao-Tzu said 'I am not as tolerant as he is.' After listening to Lao-Tzu this trader was amazed. He said 'if your students are better than you then why are they your students then? They should have been your teachers then.' Lao-Tzu smiled at the man and said, 'they all are my students because they know to be best in one quality does not qualify any individual to be called the most learned or knowledgeable, and that is why they have accepted me as their teacher.' The trader asked, 'then who is the most knowledgeable?' Lao-Tzu replied, 'that person is the most knowledgeable who has found a balance of all great qualities in him.'

Truly the best and safest thing is to keep a balance in life, acknowledge the great powers around us and in us. If you can do that and live that way, you are really a wise and balanced person.

Fortunate indeed is the man who takes exactly the right measure of himself and holds a just balance between what he can acquire and what he can use.

lao-tzu's justice

*L*ao-Tzu was a very wise person. One day emperor of China called him and said, 'You are known for your justice in China. This is why I want you to work for me on the position of the judge in this region.' Lao-Tzu tried to pursue emperor for not making him do so, but the emperor did not listen to him once. Then Lao-Tzu explained to emperor by saying 'I will be the judge for a day, first you need to see my method of doing justice if you will find it just and moral then I will work for you.' Emperor replied 'I agree to your terms and conditions.' Next day in front of him a thief was called. He had stolen money of a wealthy landlord of this region. Everyone knew that this landlord was a tyrant by nature. Lao-Tzu heard all the matter very carefully and gave his verdict 'thief and the landlord must get a six month sentence in the prison.' To hear his decision emperor and his fellow men were horrified. The landlord said 'what are you saying? This thief has stolen goods from my house. He is the rightful person to get imprisoned. Why are you sentencing me for no crime?'

Lao-Tzu said 'if I will not give you a punishment than the thief will not have justice either'. The truth is you should be punished more than this thief. You have exploited people's misery and have accumulated more wealth than needed. You keep people's land and belonging on loan and when they return your money even then you do not give it back to them. You have deprived people of their own money and wealth. People are dying of hunger but your lust for money is not ending. It is due to your own greed such thieves are there in this region. You are morally responsible for the theft taking place in your own home. You are a bigger culprit than this thief. You have to go the prison as your punishment.'

Emperor and other people present there were very pleased with Lao-Tzu's sense of justice. And the emperor appointed him as a judge in his region.

Moral

Not only criminals but people who force such crimes and criminal to become what they are should be punished equally.

a real sage

*L*ord Buddha decided to send his disciples after giving them alms and asked them to go for preaching holy sermons to various cities and villages. He told his disciples 'wherever you all will go you will face all kinds good and bad people. Good people will listen to you and will help you in obstacles, whereas bad people will criticize you. What will you feel with such behaviour?' Every disciple gave an appropriate answer to Lord Buddha according to their ability. But one of his disciples said, 'if someone will criticize me, I will not feel bad because he has just criticized me he has not slapped me at least.'

Buddha asked 'what if someone really slaps you?' Disciple said 'I will thank him because he has just slapped me he did not beat me with a stick.' 'And what if he beats you with a stick as well?' Asked Buddha. The disciple said 'I will consider he took pity on me because he did not kill me at least.' Buddha said while smiling 'and if he really kills you then what will you do?' The student answered 'there is a lot of pain in this world; if I will live longer I will have to see sufferings of others. To commit suicide is a greater sin. But if someone will free me from the misery and pain of this life I will be obliged to him in thankfulness.'

To hear his student speak in such fashion Buddha was very pleased by him. He said 'you are truly great. Only you are a true sage here. It is because a true sage never blames anyone not even in misery. I trust that you will always walk on the guided track of duty and religion.'

It is truly said that I learned the bad guys are not always bad the good guys are not always good, the one who criticizes us is not always against us. The parameters are like rules, mostly guidelines. All it takes a little bit of critisism, a little bit of bad boy to fight out in the world!

Moral

A real sage or ascetic never gets pursued by pain or troubles, he always walks on the track of humanity.

god's gift

Mishraji was counted amongst nicest of men. His desire and practice was such so that he would never land up hurting or annoying any human being he knew. But despite all efforts and all odds he would land up doing something or the other, which would make him regret his act later. One day he decided to punish himself for all his wrong doings. He decided whenever he will commit some mistake he will pluck ten hair from his scalp as his punishment. And the day there will be no hair left on his head that day he will leave this world forever. And he pledged to do so. Almost four months were gone. Mishraji was balding bit by bit. He understood by now that it was very difficult to stay away from committing mistakes. And finally such a day had come when not even a single hair on Mishraji's head was left. That day he decided to commit suicide. As soon as he was about to jump in the river he heard a voice, 'hold on it is a sin to commit suicide.' That voice was of God's messenger. Mishraji said 'but now nothing could happen. I have pledged that when a day will come when I do not have a single hair on my head I will give up my life.' To this God's messenger replied, 'you are amongst those men who have audacity to punish themselves for their own mistakes. Otherwise people do horrible things but they have no remorse for their wrong doings.'

Mishraji replied, 'everytime I saw myself balding I realised my mistakes and felt sad about them.' And again God's messenger replied to his remark, 'for your own mistakes you have punished yourself. There is no point thinking about them now. To take your sadness away God has sent a gift for you'. God's messenger gave the gift in the hands of Mishraji and vanished from the scene. As soon as Mishraji opened that gift he was amazed to see it and his eyes turned teary. There was a box which contained a hat in it for his bald head.

the rich and the poor

A very rich man was proud of his riches, whereas his own son used to consider humanity bigger than any kind of wealth. One day that rich man decided to impart in his son importance of money. He took his son with him to a village where people were quite poor. There he showed his son poverty, hunger and helplessness. After inspecting the entire scene he got his son back home. His father asked him 'so how was your excursion?'

Son replied 'yes it was very good indeed.' 'So now you know people who have no money in this world how they live or survive every day.' Said the father. 'Yes father I have seen everything.' Replied the son. Then his father asked him 'what all have you learnt from this trip tell me about it?'

Son said, 'I have seen we have one dog whereas they have many of them. Our swimming pool is somewhat small whereas they bath in a big canal. We have expensive lights to lit our house and they have entire sky full of stars to light their nights. We have servants who look after us but they take care of each other. We buy our food and they grow their own food with their hands. We have a huge boundary wall to protect our house and their neighbours look after each other's houses.' To hear all this father knew everything by now. That in reality he is a poor person not the others.

The father understood that 'if each man or woman could understand that every other human life is as full of sorrows, and joys, or base emotions, of heartaches and of remorse as his own...how much kinder, how much gentler he would be.'

Moral

A heart's fulfilment is the biggest riches and most rewarding experience of life.

misfortune

In a village lived two brothers, Radhe and Maniram. Radhe was very poor and Maniram had no scarcity of money in life. One day Radhe decided to go to a foreign land and test his destiny whether it holds something nice for him. So finally he was leaving his house to travel abroad. Then he heard someone's voice, 'I will also come along.' Radhe turned around he saw the misfortune was standing in front of him. Then misfortune spoke again, 'for so long I have been living with you. You have to take me with you.' Radhe's wife was a very smart woman. She said 'we all have some belonging or the other, you can also carry something with you, please take this flour mill which is made up of stone and put it on your head to take it with you.'

Misfortune kept that mill on its head. They all came out of the village. While walking they saw a river. Radhe's family was able to cross it, but due to the weight of heavy mill made up of stone misfortune got drowned in the river. Now Radhe's troubles with misfortune got vanished. Now his luck started to change. And bit by bit he became rich. Radhe's brother was not able to bear his good fortune. He asked about the story behind his getting rich day by day. So Radhe had to tell about all the details. Next day Maniram went to the river and somehow dragged misfortune out of the water. To have come out misfortune was extremely happy. She asked, 'how will I ever be able to pay for your kindness?' Maniram said 'just do this much return back to your old master again.'

Misfortune held Maniram's hand and said, 'what are you talking about? How could I leave such a kind and considerate man and go to live with such a bad man who tried to drown me into water, it is not possible. I cannot trust him. Maybe he will do this again.' Since that day misfortune started to live with Maniram. He became poorer day by day. To see his current situation he thought a person who makes a ditch for others can fall in it one day.

uprightness

In a village two people lived one was Sukhiya and other one was Mangoo. They were each other's neighbours as well. Sukhiya was a rich person and Mangoo was poor. One day on some matter they both had a fight with each other. The matter reached to the village head. After listening to their discord the head asked both of them to come next day. Next day when Mangoo was leaving to visit the head he had a passing thought. He thought that Sukhiya had a lot of money. If he will buy all the judges with his money then they will make their decision in his favour.

While walking he saw a very nice and shady corner. He decided to rest under the shade. Then he observed there are a lot of water melons growing in one field. On a thin and weak creeper how such heavy and big water melons could grow, by thinking so he was doubting God's creation. But he did not think much about it and decided to rest under the shade of a banyan tree. He saw fruits of the banyan tree. He said to God, 'oh Lord! This society always exploits the weak and the poor. You have also not done justice with this weak looking creeper. This frail looking creeper cannot even stand on its own. You have made that creeper bear huge melons and this huge tree on the other side can accommodate only smaller fruits. That is why a poor man thinks that when God can do such injustice than if a rich person will do so as well then what will be wrong in it.'

After a while when he got up after rest a fruit from the tree fell on his mouth. He immediately said, 'God please forgive me. Whatever you have created you have done so with uprightness. If the tree like banyan would have born fruits like water melon and if it had fallen on my head today then it would have taken my life for sure.' He felt at ease by thinking if God has not done any injustice with nature then he will not let the same happen with him. With a contented heart he approached to see the village judge.

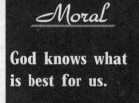

Moral

God knows what is best for us.

duty for humanity

Tetsugen was a Japanese scholar who wrote a book after the hard labour of days and nights. He wanted to get it printed but he had no money for this task. This is why he decided to accumulate money from people. He started to wander around city after city and would ask for money from the people. People who knew the value of books gave him gold coins according to their ability. There were many people who gave him silver or bronze coins as well. Tetsugen was very grateful to each one of them.

After some time Tetsugen collected more money than he required for the book. Before he could get his book printed his village river got flooded and people started to scream for help everywhere. When the calamity got over people had nothing to eat or drink. Due to this a lot of people died.

Tetsugen could not endure so much of misery around him. Whatever money he collected for getting his book printed he gave away to the flood victims. He knew that he may have worked hard to collect this money but the victims needed it the most.

Tetsugen understood that life that has been given to us as a gift is a gift of utmost preciousness. To really try to understand it, really try to recognise it is the greatest service to mankind. Through the media of this knowledge, we can tap into our inner resources that is capable of giving us most happiness; to us as well as to others.

Moral

A person who does not consider his own self at the time of distress is the greatest human being.

three sages

*I*n search of knowledge three sages reached the summit of Himalaya. When they reached there they grew very hungry. When they looked around they found out they had only two roti with them. Three of them decided they will sleep hungry tonight and if God will come in one of their dreams that person will eat those two roti.

Three sages slept then and there. When the night was at its final stage they all got up and started narrating their dreams to each other. The first one said 'I reached to an unknown place. There was a lot of peace. And I found God as well. He said to me that- you have always scarified a lot in life therefore you must eat those roti.' The second one started narrating his own dream, he said 'I saw in my dream that in the past when I was worshiping I became an enlightened soul and I met God. He said to me for worshiping so much I have the authority on these two roti to be eaten and it should not be given to my friends.'

Third one said 'I have seen nothing in my dream, because I have eaten those two roti.' To hear this both the sages were very angry. They said to the third one, 'before taking this decision why you did not wake us that moment?' third one said 'how I could have woken you two up because you both were busy talking to the God himself. But God woke me up and saved me from dying of hunger.' It is wisely said if the question is about live and death then no one is a friend in such a situation. A person does that thing first which can save his life.

Life is such a precious gift. Whatever life throws at us, if we could just learn to get through that day and hang on to the next, you never know what may come. It may get worse, but you never know.

Moral

In front of hunger even biggest holy and dutiful men can leave their faith.

foot steps

There was a villager whose name was Deendayal. One day a sagacious man arrived in his village. Deendyal went to hear his holy sermons. He got very influenced by this saint's sermons. He thought he will also spend his life in solving life's mysteries and he will follow this sainnt's footsteps. For many years he was seen in the garb of an ascetic. He will roam around like him but he did not feel any change occurring in him and neither could he solve the mystery of human life. This made him very sad.

One night in his dream he had an audience with God himself. And he asked, 'Deendyal, why are you so unhappy?' Deendyal said, 'Dear Lord! I am old now. My life can be over any moment now. But still I haven't found out all the secrets of human life. I did not get enlightenment like that saint.' God replied, 'every human being has his own quality and identity. If you would have lived your whole life as being Deendyal only then you would have found some truth or the other. But you have spent all your life being like that saint only. When you will be coming to me some day I may not ask you how good a saint you were but I how good a human being you had been. Give up the idea of being a saint now try being a good human being.'

In everyone's life, at some time our inner fire goes out. It may then burst into flame by an encounter with another human being. We should all be thankful for those people who rekindle the inner spirit. Safeguarding the rights of others is the most noble and beautiful end of a human being.

> **Moral**
> It is wiser to be good human being than imitating another mortal soul. God is happier to know that a person is a good mortal soul.

a change in conduct

There was a man named Dhaniram, he was very worried due to his wife's miserliness. Her name was Kaushalya. Despite his desire to spend he couldn't. One day he was passing through a market place feeling helpless and desponded, when he met his old friend Sundar in the market. After meeting each other after a long time they both started to catch up with each others progress in life and business.

After a while their topic shifted towards their wives. Sundar started to praise his wife. When he asked Dhaniram about his wife he said, 'in my wife Kaushalya there are a lot of good qualities, but due to her miserliness all her good qualities get drowned somehow. Since the time I have married her I have seen this bad habit in her. I do not know how to explain to her that sometimes it is alright to spend money for enjoyment also.'

After listening to him, Sundar asked Dhaniram to take him to his house. He did the same. There in front of Kaushalya he made a fist and asked her, 'if my fist remains like this in the same position, then what would you call it?' Kaushalya said 'I will think as if your hand is paralysed.' Now Sundar open his fist and said if my hand remains like this what would you think it about it?' Kaushalya replied, 'I will think again your hand does not move fully therefore it is paralysed.' Then Sundar said 'you are also a victim of a certain kind of paralysis.'

Kaushalya remarked, 'I do not understand what are you saying?' He replied, 'it is simple. If your hand stays in same position you will feel as if it is paralysed. This is why I said your behaviour has got paralysed. Since the time of our marriage you have shown one behaviour only, which is miserliness. If you are fine in your health then change your behaviour as well.' Having said this Sundar left that place. Kaushalya was very clever. She understood what Sundar had said and she left her bad habit of being a miser. Now she could save and spend as well.

Moral
To save things or money is a good habit, but miserliness is almost a disease. One must eradicate such a disease.

a king's sacrifice

Somgardh's king Sher Singh was always drenched in fun and frolic. On the other hand Ramgardh's king Ram Singh used to love his people and his kingdom a lot. To see Ramgardh flourishing and its people happy used to make Sher Singh feel jealous. One day his jealousy crossed its boundary and he attacked Ramgardh. Ram Singh thought if I will go for the war then my innocent soldiers will have to lose their lives. Without going for war he gave all his kingdom to Sher Singh and he went to a jungle and lived in a cave.

One day two wood cutters came around his cave to gather wood, their names were Ramu and Shamu. Ramu said to Shamu, 'Sher Singh has announced anyone who can bring Ram Singh to his court will be given a reward of ten thousand gold coins. If we will get those gold coins then our poverty will be taken care of.' After listening to their talk Ram Singh came out of his cave and said, 'if you can become rich because of me then I am more than willing to come with you.'

Two of them took him to Sher Singh. Sher Singh gave the due reward to both the boys and bid them farewell, and he embraced Ram Singh. To see this entire court was amazed and surprised. Sher Singh spoke, 'whatever pain I have caused you I am sorry for that. Now you must take care of your kingdom and throne. I have learnt that on the basis of power and might one can take over a kingdom but cannot win people's heart and faith. In future as well I will try to keep my people happy.' To have said this Sher Singh returned his kingdom Somgardh to Ram Singh.

It is said that we have flown the air like birds and swum the seas like fishes, but have yet to learn the simple fact of walking the earth like brothers.

Moral

You should always be ready to help others.

the mountain has bowed down

Once king Chitrasen was going to a battle with his army. The track he chose to travel had a huge mountain along the way. As soon as king was ready to climb this mountain he heard a voice coming. He turned around and saw an old woman standing there. She said, 'a lot many heroes and brave men tried to cross this mountain. And they all have given up their lives in this pursuit. And so far no one has been successful in doing so.'

King said, 'what you told me has encouraged me further to do so. I would show such an act which no one has been able to perform so far.' The old woman tried to explain to him once more, but this king did not listen to her. He said, 'once I decide to do something then I never return back from my aim. Even if I die, my bravery and goodness will live after me.'

King commanded his army, 'Proceed! Think there is no mountain on our track. We have to fight with the army standing on it. Just keep one's enemies in mind.' To listen to their king speak, entire army got ready to march ahead on that mountain. King Chitrasen was right in front of them. In the end they conquered their enemies and that mountain as well and gained victory.

It is wisely said if a human being gets scared by listening to others, then he would never succeed ever in life. For a brave and determined human being a difficult summit can turn into an easy walk.

To sum up, conquest is the mission of valour and the hard impact of military virtues beats the meanness out of the world. True valour or virtue founded strong, overcomes all events alike.

pearls of offerings

One day Guru Ramdev was engrossed in his meditation on the bank of a river. That moment a student of his arrived. He showed his devotion and submission in front of him. He placed two precious pearls right next to his feet. This was his offering for his teacher. Guru felt something was touching his feet, so he opened his eyes and asked, 'what all is this happening?'

His student replied, 'guru this is my offering for you which as a student I am required to pay. Kindly accept it.' The guru picked up both the pearls in his hands and suddenly one of it slipped from his hands and fell in the river, and the student also dived in the river to fetch the pearl out. He kept looking for it but did not get it. When he got out of water he said to guru, 'you must have seen where that pearl fell, if you could tell me the exact spot then I can find it easily.'

Guru picked up another pearl and threw it at the same spot where the first one fell and said, 'that is the place where that pearl has fallen.' By seeing guru do so student understood that those pearls might be valuable for him but for the guru they hold no importance. He understood that an object he was giving as his offering was not needed at all in the teacher's life.

We should know that if everyone demanded peace instead of another television set, then there would be peace in the world. A lot of people get so hung up on what they have that they don't think for a second about what they really need for peace and happiness.

Moral

The knowledge which a teacher imparts is most precious and no one can pay back it's worth.

the seventh urn

There was a trader. He used to bring goods from a city and sell it in the village. Like every day he was going to the city by taking a different route he saw a cave. When he was inside this cave he noticed seven urns were lying there. He opened the urns. They all were filled with gold coins. But the seventh one was half full and there was a paper placed inside that urn. The paper read 'Beware the one who finds these urns! The person who will take them will never be able to find happiness in this wealth.'

Greed by now has seized the mind of this trader. Without any delay he arranged for these urns to be carried towards his home. All the time he adored his new found urns and was dreaming about a comfortable life full of every possibility. But as soon as he would think about the seventh urn he would feel bad about the fact it was half full. He decided to fill the remaining half of this urn by working hard. He thought till the time he would fill the other half of this urn he will not take out money from any of these urns.

From next day onwards he was working twice as much as before. Whatever he would earn he would land up exchanging that money for gold and would put in the seventh urn. This is how a lot of years have passed but the seventh urn was not getting filled somehow. No matter how much of gold he would put in the seventh urn it would remain half empty like ever. For working so hard and not being able to pay attention on his health trader fell severely ill. And after some time he died. During his last moments he was thinking whatever wealth he had was enough to spend his life comfortably. But he was blinded by greed and tried to fill the seventh urn throughout. He had so much of money but yet he could not attain any happiness out of it. And whatever wealth a human being has it is somehow never enough.

Moral

To have a desire for more wealth never gets satiated.

the circle of greed

*I*n a village lived a woodcutter whose name was Thumban. One day his wife said that we have spent our live just like this, and you have hardly seen what lies ahead in the forest. Thumban felt bad with his wife's remark. That day he went far, far ahead from the spot where he used to cut trees every day. Thumban must have walked about a mile and he noticed a mine of bronze. He grew very happy and he started to sell bronze by taking it from this place. His wife started to bicker again about proceeding from this bronze mine and this time he found out silver mine. Now he started to sell silver from this mine and started having a good life.

Now his wife said again, 'if you will go further maybe you will get gold as well.' And that happened as well. Now he would go once in a while to just roam around and whenever he felt a need he would bring the gold in order to sell it. And one day again his wife made a complain to which he said, 'what you desire after this?' Even then he went and this time he was lucky to find a diamond mine. He picked so many diamonds in one go that he could spend his life very comfortably. When he reached home he told his wife 'now this much of wealth would be enough for our life. Even our next seven generations could survive on this money.' But his wife was not satisfied. Therefore Tumban went further and went ahead of the diamond mine, but this time came to the same place from where he has started from. His house was broken like before and his wife was sitting wearing old worn out clothes like before and she was cursing greediness. Thumban sighed and said, 'in a way it is good now one circle of greed got over.' Like before he was content in going to the forest forcutting the woods like before.

Truly, greed is the bottomless pit which exhausts the person in an endless effort to satisfy the need without ever reaching satisfaction.

Moral

Greed puts people in trouble and creates more misery.

knowledge

There was one highly knowledgeable and learned hermit. Two young boys came to seek his permission in order to be his students, but this hermit has never made anyone his student before. But both the boys were adamant in being his disciple, therefore the hermit decided to test them. He gave two stones to both the boys and instructed them to place it at such a place where no one could see them. Both the boys kept their stones in their fists and walked in two different directions to follow hermit's instruction. One boy found out one isolated spot and dug the stone in the ground. Second one was not able to do so. He returned while holding the same stone in his fist and came back to the hermit

The first boy assured the hermit that he has placed that stone at such a place where no one would be able to see it at all, and neither anyone saw him doing so. Second boy shared his difficulty and told he could not find such a spot. And there was no such place where he was not visible. He said whether anybody could see him or not but God was looking all the time at him.

After listening to the first boy the hermit said, 'certainly you are not fit to become my student. Therefore go from here.' And told the second one, 'indeed you are the most knowledgeable one therefore you do not need my guidance because you already have seen God in his every manifestation.' They both understood one fact which was a person who sees God in all forms does not need to be a student of any hermit.

It is true that God is everywhere but he is most manifest in man. So serve man as God. That's as good as worshipping God.

Moral

God is everywhere and he is omnipotent. A person who knows this is considered knowledgeable. He does not need spiritual guidance.

wealth of knowledge

To witness guru Nagarjun's wisdom a thief arrived to see him one day. He told the guru, 'I would like to become you disciple. But by profession I am a thief and I cannot leave stealing. But still can you make me your student?' Guru said 'who is putting an end to your stealing habit?' Thief felt bizarre after listening to this guru. Then he could not resist and asked, 'before you whenever I have approached anyone for being their student they all asked to take me in on one condition which was I must give up stealing forever. But this habit of mine did not bother you at all?'

Guru said, 'you must have gone to them in order to steal something from them, which is why they must have put this condition on you. But to me you actually come to be my disciple. And I am able to see you as my student not as a thief. Now go from here, I declare you my student and do as you please. But remember one thing whatever you do, do it with a conscience mind.'

This thief left the place and came after a long time and said, 'that day I did not understand your words, but today I have understood it. That day when you have asked me to be conscious of what I do because you knew I will not be able to steal anymore and will return to you.' The guru smiled, 'but why? What peculiar thing has happened with you?' This thief replied 'last night I went inside the king's palace to steal. As soon as I opened his safe I saw a lot of money. I could have stolen it and would have become rich but, I do not know what happened to me that moment. All that money and gems were appearing like stone to me. That moment I knew what I will be receiving by becoming your disciple in front of that knowledge this wealth is nothing. The real wealth is knowledge itself.'

Ordinary riches can be stolen, real riches cannot. In your soul are infinitely precious things that cannot be taken from you.

Moral

Nothing is bigger than knowledge in this world.

40

value of money or of knowledge

One day king Ratansingh came for hunting to the forest. In order to look for a prey he went far ahead. All his men and helper were left behind. Even his horse grew vary of distance and was extremely tired. Even king was feeling very thirsty. Then he saw two boys who were there to feed the cattle. King asked them, 'me and my horse are very thirsty. Can you provide some water to drink?' both the boys arranged for water immediately.

King was very happy with their services and invited them both to his court in order to give him a reward. Next day both the boys arrived in the royal court. King said to them they can ask for their desired wish in order to seek this reward. They both had no cattle of their own and nor a piece of land.

That is why a boy asked for some cattle and a piece of land as his reward. Now it was the turn of another boy to ask for something. He said, 'due to poverty my parents could not educate me. I want to be a smart and clever man after getting proper education.' The king gave cattle and land to the first one and bid him a goodbye and kept the second boy with him and gave him full education. After acquiring education when the boy grew up king bestowed on him the charge of one of the villages to govern.

In future there was a famine the first boy's cattle died and he had to sell his land as well. Whereas the second boy who was made in charge lived his life well because of his smartness and good choice.

Education in the most powerful weapon which you can use to charge the world. It is thousand times better to have commonsense without education than to have education without commonsense.

85

fragrance of the hands

Mohan used to visit a temple every day. Right outside the temple there used to sit flower sellers. Mohan used to buy flowers from that shop regularly. And the flower seller was very happy and a chirpy fellow. People were always keen to buy garlands from his shop. Once Mohan met a big loss in his business. He felt sad and depressed. To make up for the loss he had to mortgage his big house and live in a smaller house. But his financial condition was getting worst. All day and night he was consumed by the thought of his losses. He could not think straight in order to know what he must do and what he should not do. A lot of people suggested to start a new business which required lesser money, but Mohan did not feel up for a smaller work. One day he went to the temple to keep his sadness in front of God.

He saw right next to the temple the flower seller was selling flowers with a big smile. Mohan cannot resist and asked him, 'do you not have any kind of pain or sadness? How you manage to laugh so much?' The flower seller said, 'I agree that I have a very good line of work. In a way I distribute flowers and the people who receive them their hands always smell nice with fragrance.' Mohan found out a solution of his problems, that is not any work is small or big but our thinking makes it so.

Whoever is careless with the truth in small matters cannot be trusted with important matters.

a stupid, foolish conch

In a village lived a man whose name was Bhagatram. He was a very poor man. But he would remain immersed in God's meditation. His prime work was to sing devotional songs and chants for the villagers in praise of God. In return whatever minimal things villagers would offer him could not satisfy his basic needs of everyday life. Due to which his wife would hurl curses at him. One day Bhagatram finally became totally sad by these absuses. He went to the jungle and decided to sit is deep meditation renouncing the world.

God was very happy and pleased by his devotion and gave him a boon. He gave Bhagatram a conch and said whatever he wishes he has will be fulfilled if he will blows this conch. Having received such a boon Bhagatram was very elated and returned back to his home. Now all his needs were met with the help of that conch shell. With more devotion than before he started to worship and pray to God. With his better life and well-being, his neighbour Shayamlal became jealous. He wanted to know the secret.

When he got to know about this magical conch shell, he plotted a scheme to steal it. One night Shyamlal stole that conch. Bhagatram was worried to know his source of livelihood has been lost. The loss troubled him. To see him worried God bestowed even a bigger and better conch shell on to him. The bigger conch said in a hoarse voice, 'what good quality lies in that small shell? I can give you twice as much as that small shell.' To hear this Shyamlal became greedier. He went to Bhagatram's house and placed the smaller shell back again and took the bigger one from there.

Whenever Shyamlal would ask for a wish that big conch used to brag about giving him hundred times more than ever, but would give nothing in return, now Shyamlal was annoyed to hear mere talks of that foolish conch shell. When he started to curse Bhagatram then that stupid conch replied, 'Bhagatram's conch is real and I am just stupid and foolish, I give nothing but can make a lot of noise.'

Moral

Never to brag about anything. Whatever you say must do it well.

a valuable treasure

In a mountainous region a woman lived in a village. One day she was crossing a hill in order to go back to her house. Suddenly she noticed something shiny was lying there on the track. She went near that object; she saw it was a precious gem. She picked it up and kept it in her bag. After a while on the same road at a distance she found a traveller who was very hungry. As soon as the woman has put her hand inside her bag this strange man saw her precious jewel and snatched it from this woman's hand. This woman did not say anything for this act of his. Rather she gave him blessings. And she walked ahead happily.

The traveller felt very strange. He took that precious gem and walked ahead. Few days went just like that and this man kept on wondering how did that woman let him have this precious gem without any complain and she gave it happily. He thought did she not know its actual worth? This matter caused him discomfort. He went looking for that woman and came to her in order to return that gem and said, 'I know that this gem is very precious, even then I am here to return it to you.' To hear him talk like this woman was astounded. She asked 'but why are you returning it to me?'

Traveller said, 'this gem belongs only to you. I want that precious treasure which is hiding inside you. Teach me to perform good deeds. You have such a precious quality in you in front of which all the riches of this world will diminish. And we human beings cannot realise this quality in us and we run behind fake riches and wealth of this world.'

The moment I realise God is sitting in the temple of every human body, the moment I stand in reverence before every human being and see God in him/her–that moment I am free from bondage of any material riches, everything that binds us vanishes and am free.

Moral

A person's true richness lies in his or her goodness, scarifies, humanity and honesty. In front of these qualities all the money and riches are worthless.

11

controlling anger

In a village lived a farmer named Balu. He had a son who was around ten or eleven years old, whose name was Gopal. Gopal used to be angry much of the time. On small matters he would get enraged and start beating up as well. Balu tried explaining to him but nothing came out of it. One day Balu said while giving his son a bag full of nails, 'son whenever you get angry hammer a nail on the tree right outside our house. The day you control your anger fully and do not hammer a single nail on the tree that day tell me about it.'

First day Gopal hammered three nails on the tree. Things like this went or for a few days. Finally a day arrived when Gopal did not hammer a single nail on that tree. That day he went to his father and said, 'father! I have controlled my anger. Today I have not hammered a single nail on that tree.' After listening to him Balu said 'now take out all the nails from the tree.' And Gopal did the same as his father asked. He took out all the nails from that tree.

Balu addressed his son and said, 'you have done a great thing by taking care of your anger. Now whenever you get angry go and see the trunk of that tree. It has all those marks on it. And the same kind of marks you leave behind on people's heart when you say nasty things to them out of your anger. Later you can seek their forgiveness but you cannot heal those wounds. This is why with your intention, speech and knowledge never ever commit such an act which you will have to repent for rest of your life.'

If you must speak ill or bad of another, do not speak it, write it in the sand near the water's edge. In course of time wind or water will wash it away. But if you speak ill, it will be engraved as if on a stone and no amount of repentance will ever be able to wash if away.

Moral
To get enraged by anger and ask for forgiveness does not take care of hurt. It is also a sinful act. And the scars caused by it never gets healed.

the tour of heaven and hell

One day Bholuram passed away. When he met God he said, 'God! I would like to see heaven and hell both. Would you be kind enough to show me both?' God replied, 'Sure come with me.' God took him to a place where there were two doors of the same kind. God opened first door and they entered that place. Bholuram saw a big table was lying there. The world's best cuisine was served on that table but, all the people sitting there were looking thin and emaciated. It appeared as if they have not eaten for past few days now.

They were holding big spoons in their hands. Those spoons were so long that it was nearly impossible to eat from such spoons. To see them Bholuram was pitying their fate. Then suddenly God opened another door. In that room was also a big table, and it had best food served on it as well. All the people sitting there were looking healthy. Then Bhuloram asked 'they all have such big spoons in their hands as well. They would be having difficulty in eating from those spoons. Even then these people are healthy looking if compared to those people we saw earlier. After all how can these people eat from such long spoons?'

God said it is fairly simple, 'in heaven people feed each other with such big spoons this is why they all are quite healthy and happy. In hell people are selfish and self-absorbed. They don't think about others and only mean bad for each other, this is why they look unhealthy and sad. They keep on trying to eat from that big spoon and can never eat anything at all.' To hear God say this Bholuram thought, it is true those people who stay and share together are always happy and live a healthy life.

It is believed that hard times hit all of us at some time. Let us enjoy our fortune; let our fortune help others; people helping people makes this world a better place.

Moral

One must leave how to show things with others.

a wooden trunk

Ramsukh was a very hardworking farmer. But now he had become old. He could barely work in fields any more. He would go every day to his farm and after working for a short time start to feel tired and then he would sit under a tree to rest. Whenever his son Bhola would see his father resting he used to think, he could not work vigorously any longer therefore there is no need for him in life. One day Bhola made a wooden trunk which was quite big. He asked Ramsukh to sit inside this trunk and he silently sat inside that trunk. Bhola dragged that trunk somehow towards the mountain top. As soon as he was about to push the trunk of the cliff he heard that Ramsukh was knocking it from inside.

Bhola opened the trunk. Ramsukh said, 'I know you are about to throw me from this cliff. And before you do this I want to tell you something. Keep this trunk safe and intact because when you will grow old it will be of help to your children.' To hear his father talk like this Bhola's eyes got open. He knew by now one day his children might as well do the same as he is doing with his father today. He opened that trunk and took his father out and asked for forgiveness. Ramsukh embraced his son and he forgave him.

It is said that when you hold resentment toward another, you are bound to that person or condition by an emotional link that is stronger than steel. Forgiveness is the only way to dissolve that link and get free.

> **Moral**
> The same kind of behaviour you younger ones will do with you as you do with your elders, we must always keep this in mind.

lakshmi has to go

There was a rich man called Karorimal. Like his name he was a very wealthy man himself. Goddess Lakshmi was very merciful on him. He grew very proud of his wealth. One night Goddess Lakshmi came in his dream and said-'Karorimal! You are a very rich man. This is why you have become very proud now. I am going to leave you for some days and going across Ganges to be with Fakira the sweet maker. Now nothing will be left with you.'

After listening to her in dreams he woke up suddenly. The very next day he tried to hide all his money in the attic of his house. But it was his time to suffer a bad luck. After few days an earth quake came and his house fell apart with the attic. Everything fell even the metal beams of his house and got drowned in Ganges and went afloat towards the extreme shore. When on the other end a boatman named Bulaki saw those beams lying on the shore he thought of making money out of them by selling them off. He sold those beams to Fakira the sweet seller. When Fakira gave those metal beams to a black smith to break into pieces, he found out gold coins were stuffed in them. Fakira took all gold coins and came to his house.

On the other side of the river, the wealthy man was miserable now and had no money to feed him anymore. He knew that his wealth now has reached to Fakira. He decided to meet Fakira and request him to return his wealth. He packed two portions of bread and left home. Bulaki the boatmen made him cross Ganges and asked for the fair. Karorimal said 'I have two portions of bread, one you can take from me.' Boatman agreed to his terms. After crossing Ganges Karorimal went to see Fakira. Fakira felt sorry for him and gave him two sweets in return. And he hid two gold coins in them. Karorimal left his place and went towards Ganges to be taken by boatman. When boatman asked for the boat fair he grew disappointed and offered him both the sweets which had gold coins in them. When he returned back on his shore Bulaki decided to sell them to Fakira in lieu of money. That is why it is said where Goddess Lakshmi and her wealth will go it will decide its own course.

Moral

The bounties of wealth come with a lot of luck and pre-ordination.

debt

Two strangers were passing from the deserts of Rajasthan. On their way the night fell after walking all day. They thought they must stay at one place and get some sleep during the night. To stay they were finding a suitable place then suddenly they saw house. They went to the house and knocked its door. The house's owner Sohanlal came out. To see two strangers at his door he asked, 'who are you? And what are you doing here so late at night?' the strangers replied, 'we are travellers and we want a place to stay for the night and it is already late. If you do not have any problem can we stay here over-night.'

Sohanlal asked them to come in with a lot of respect and whatever was in the house he offered them to eat. And the travellers slept after having their food. Next day they both woke up early as well. They washed their hands and faces and got ready to leave but left some money right next to Sohanlal who was sleeping. They just reached a certain distance they heard a scream, 'Stop now!' when they turned around they saw Sohanlal was running towards them. To see him they both stopped.

Sohanlal came towards them and said while catching his breath, 'why you both have left so suddenly? Did I do something wrong?' they replied, 'no there wasn't anything wrong friend! You did a lot for us. We have to reach our destination soon. This is why we left.' Then Sohanlal said while giving their money back, 'in a hurry you have left this money at my house. This is what I wanted to return to you.' Then the travellers said, 'but we left this money for you Sohanlal.' Sohanlal said, 'but I do not need it. Do you want to pay back for my hospitality and affection which I have showed to you? Even if you want you cannot do so. The travellers understood what Sohanlal meant. They knew by now, a person who helps someone in times of need his gratitude can never be paid back. They took money from him and said thanks to Sohanlal and went ahead.

Moral

One cannot payback the gratitude of humanity and hospitality showed to a person in times of need.

god's grace

On the coast of a sea there was a fishing village. One day all fishermen went in the sea on their boats to catch some fish. When they were about to return a sea storm came. And all fishermen went astray from the set direction.

In the village their families were praying to God for their safe return. They all were quite distressed. Suddenly the lightning struck one fisherman's house and the house caught fire. All fishermen's families were near the sea and no one was in the village that time therefore no one was able to extinguish the fire in time. In the morning everyone was happy to know all fishermen had arrived safely and anchored their boats on the shore. And the fisherman whose house caught fire, his wife told entire story while crying. The fisherman replied, 'I am sad to learn the house is burnt, but to see that burning house we understood where and how far the land was last night.' To hear him say this, his wife stopped crying and she said her graces for God. Next day all fishermen united in the village to make a new hut for them.

God's action are beyond our comprehension. Nicholas Sparks said that I have faith that God will show you the answer. But you have to understand that sometimes it takes a while to be able to recognise what God wants. That's how it often is. God's voice is usually nothing more than a whisper and you have to listen very carefully to hear it. But at other times in those rarest of moments the answer is obvious and rings as loud as a bell.

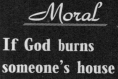

Moral

If God burns someone's house then he shows the light to someone as well.

a sinner's well

One holy man was crossing the jungles to go for a pilgrimage. While walking he felt thirsty. At one place he saw a well. When he reached he saw a rope and a bucket tied to one end there. The holy man hurriedly threw the rope and the bucket in the well to draw water and drank it in a hurry. After quenching his thirst he felt a need to take away the water filled bucket with him along the way. He felt if he will have water then it will be good for him. Whenever he will feel thirsty he will drink the water. When he looked around there was no one to ask or say anything to him. The holy man lowered the bucket again in the well and drew water from it. When he was un-tying the rope from the bucket then a voice came, 'Don't! Are you trying to steal it from here?'

To hear this holy man was shocked. He thought how did an idea of stealing something has entered his mind. Leaving the water and bucket behind he reached inside the kingdom of that king where he was standing at the moment. He asked the king, 'there is a well in your kingdom; it is constructed out of whose wealth?' When the king enquired about it he learnt it was made by a thief. When he was caught with his confiscated money he got this well made as a punishment as well as repentance. Then the holy man said, 'he must have saved all that money after stealing and burglary. This is the reason why I had a sudden pang of greed in my heart after drinking water from it and wanted to steal the bucket of this well.'

It is said that if there is one realm in which it is essential to be sublime, it is in wickedness. You spit on a petty thief, but you can't deny a kind of respect for this criminal.

Moral
A person who uses another person's object or wealth gets influenced by him in similar fashion

 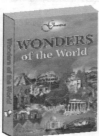